MARIJUANA STOCKS

Insider Secrets - 15 High Growth Potential Pot Stocks That Need to Be on Your Radar

© Copyright 2020 - All rights reserved.

The content contained within this book may not be reproduced, duplicated or transmitted without direct written permission from the author or the publisher.

Under no circumstances will any blame or legal responsibility be held against the publisher, or author, for any damages, reparation, or monetary loss due to the information contained within this book, either directly or indirectly.

Legal Notice:

This book is copyright protected. It is only for personal use. You cannot amend, distribute, sell, use, quote or paraphrase any part, or the content within this book, without the consent of the author or publisher.

Disclaimer Notice:

Please note the information contained within this document is for educational and entertainment purposes only. All effort has been executed to present accurate, up to date, reliable, complete information. No warranties of any kind are declared or implied. Readers acknowledge that the author is not engaged in the rendering of legal, financial, medical or professional advice. The content within this book has been derived from various sources. Please consult a licensed professional before attempting any techniques outlined in this book.

By reading this document, the reader agrees that under no circumstances is the author responsible for any losses, direct or indirect, that are incurred as a result of the use of the information contained within this document, including, but not limited to, errors, omissions, or inaccuracies.

Table of Contents:

Introduction: Marijuana Matters 8
Chapter 1: Why 2020 is a Good Time to Buy Marijuana Stocks. 12
   What Does This Mean for Pot Stocks? 18
Chapter 2: Top 5 Marijuana Investing Mistakes and How to Avoid Them 21
   #1. Putting All Your Eggs in One Basket 22
   #2. Putting Your Eggs in Too Many Baskets 23
   #3. Guessing Instead of Researching 25
      Don't Only Buy What's Popular 25
      Don't Focus Too Much on Price 26
   #4. Don't Jump the Gun 28
   #5. Buying in Based on Hype 30
   Choose Wisely 32
Chapter 3: Risks in Investing in Marijuana Stocks 33
   Laws May Affect Trading 34
   It Might Not Pan Out 35
   Commoditization 37
   Dilution 38
   Financial Backing May Be Scarce 39
   Are the Risks Worth It? 40
Chapter 4: These Two Marijuana Stocks Could Be the Biggest Winners in 2020 42
   Planet 13 Holdings Inc 43
      (OTCMKTS:PLNHF, CNSX:PLTH). 43
      Why It's Worth Watching 44
   GrowGeneration Corp 45
      (NASDAQ:GRWG) 45
      Why It's Worth Watching 45

Which Should You Pick? 46
Chapter 5: Two Pot Stocks You Should Avoid in 2020 47
   CanopyGrowth 48
      (NYSE:CGC) 48
   CronosGroup 50
      (NASDAQ:CRON) 50
   What If You Choose to Invest Anyway? 51

Chapter 6: 15 High Potential Marijuana Stocks that Could Make You Rich Quick 53
   If You Want to Play it Safe: 55
      Curleaf Industries (CURLF) 55
      Innovative Industrial Properties (IIPR).......... 56
      cbdMD (YBD) 56
      Truelieve Cannabis (TCNFF) 57
      GW Pharmaceuticals (GWPH) 58
      Honorable Mention: iAnthus Capital Holdings (CNSX) 58
   Medium-Risk Pot Stocks: 59
      Harvest Health and Recreation (HRVSF) 59
      Green Thumb Industries (GTBIF) 59
      Aphria (APHA) 60
      Sprott Inc. (SII) 60
      The Valens Co. (VLNS) 61
   High-Risk, High-Gain Stocks: 62
      Emerald Health Therapeutics (EMHTF) 63
      Acreage Holdings (ACRGF) 63
      Hexo (HEXO) 64
      MariMed (MRMD) 65
   A Word of Warning 65

Chapter 7: What Investors Need to Know About Marijuana Real Estate 67
   What is Marijuana Real Estate? 68
   Laws You Should Be Aware Of 69
   What Does This Mean for Investors? 71
   Which Real Estate Should You Invest In? 73

Chapter 8: The Best 3 "Not-Quite-Marijuana" Pot Stocks 75
   Charlotte's Web (CWBHF) 77
   AbbVie (ABBV) 78
   Aleafia (ALEAF) 79
      Honorable Mentions 79
   Ancillary Pot Stocks 80
      KushCo Holdings (KSHB) 80
   Which Market Should You Invest In? 81

Chapter 9: If More States Legalize Marijuana in 2020, This Stock Could Be the Biggest Winner 83
   Marijuana Itself Could Be the Victor 84
   Real Estate May Be the Winner 85
   Ancillary Is the True Victor 86
   These Stocks Have the Most Potential................ 87
      Scott's Miracle Gro (SMG) 89
      Why Not Kushco, Then? 90

Conclusion: 2020 Could Be the Year for You 92

References 97

FREE BONUS

As a gift to you for purchasing my book I'm offering a special bonus - a free report relieving 3 Marijuana Penny Stocks with huge growth potential in 2020. These 3 Pot Stocks could be a big win for smart investors both in a short or long term.

Scan this QR code to get a Free Report

Introduction: Marijuana Matters

The world still has a long way to go before marijuana is fully accepted, and more importantly, integrated into society. Recent statistics show that the majority of countries still enforce laws against it, while only a handful have totally legalized it—for both recreational and medicinal use (Countries Where Weed Is Illegal, 2019).

Legalization is a hot topic right now. People want the right to enjoy their pot—for whichever reason—without the stigma of being a drug addict, loser or criminal. It seems that when talks of legalization and decriminalization come into play, it's always from the perspective of one of two sides; those who want to use it recreationally, and those who need it for medical reasons. But there's a whole new facet to placing it in the mainstream—one that the world hasn't really woken up to yet: commercial marijuana.

If you're fortunate enough to live in a country (or state) where "Mary-Jane" has been fully legalized, you now have ample opportunity to make good money through its trade. Marijuana stocks are beginning to boom, those who still don't see marijuana as a valuable commodity are missing out on. However, I must warn you that if you're only looking into this because—no offense—you're a pothead and you want to live your very own *Jay and Silent Bob* adventure, marijuana stocks aren't for you. This is business. If you don't approach trading with the mindset of a business person, you're going to set yourself up for failure.

At the end of the day, it's still marijuana; meaning that only a fraction of the world has accepted it as a legitimate commodity, as mentioned previously. So, finding information on how and when to invest or trade can be tricky. That's why I've compiled this book. I'll walk you through it and point you in the right direction, but remember... You can lead a horse to water, but you can't make it drink.

You won't find justifications for your interest in marijuana here. This is not a textbook essay on why it should be legalized, or how it aids those who need it. This is a business book that will teach you how to make money if you're serious about doing so.

That said, your very first step is to understand the commercial climate that marijuana lives in. If trading marijuana isn't new to you, you may be wondering if it's still worth it, now that the hype of its legalization in certain countries has worn off.

Well, yes, it is. Predictions for marijuana stocks are promising in the coming years, with an expected compound annual growth rate (CAGR) of 35.5 percent by 2026 (Medgadget, 2020). This means that it's expected to bring in approximately 155 billion dollars by then. Forecasters are expecting the market to surge in 2020 as well, particularly in Canada and the United States, as more products enter the market, and more states legalize cannabis.

Before you go rushing off to throw your money at marijuana, the next thing you need is to understand how the market is set up. In a nutshell, there are four types of stocks.

- **Distribution and Retail:** Likely the most popular type, this is the sort most people are drawn to. Here, one party cultivates and harvests marijuana with the intention of selling it to customers, regardless of whether they're using it recreationally or medicinally.

- **Biotechs:** Largely involves corporations who trade marijuana for its use in medicine. This typically has to do with engineering cannabinoid pharmaceuticals. GW Pharmaceuticals is a good example of this division.

- **Ancillary:** Deals with the supplementary products and equipment that go alongside cultivating (or using) marijuana, like hydroponic equipment, lighting and grow tents.
- **Real Estate:** The most complicated of the four, cannabis real estate is exactly what it sounds like; the property used to conduct marijuana business. This could be land for growing, or a retail store to fulfill customer orders.

These are the four stocks that you should pay attention to if you want to make sufficient profits in 2020 and moving forward. I will return to them as necessary, but I encourage you to research the ones that interest you to the best of your ability beyond this book.

Once you connect the dots between the rising marijuana market and the trades that are shining front and center, you'll be well on your way to successful trading within this niche.

The final step in preparing to trade would be to study the stock market and get to know marijuana's place in it. I can help you there. Your first lesson is getting to know the stocks as they are right now in 2020. You're about to see how high their value can be.

Chapter 1:
Why 2020 is a Good Time to Buy Marijuana Stocks.

Despite the COVID-19 market crush, most people, forecasters included, have a feeling that 2020 is going to be an important year for pot stocks. I must, of course, give you the disclaimer that no one can tell the future and if you choose to invest in any stocks (at any given time) it is at your own risk—but no one can deny things are looking good for those who want to get into trading marijuana this year and this decade. There are quite a few factors that push us to believe this, most of which are centered around what's happening (or likely to happen) in the United States.

The first big push towards better things was the legalization of recreational marijuana in Illinois, which took effect on January 1 (Gould & Berke, 2019). It sounds like a simple change, but the implications are huge.

Illinois became the second midwestern state to climb on board the legalization train. This means that the value of marijuana is spreading to corners of the USA no one ever thought it would. While it's unlikely that everyone in Illinois has a use for cannabis, that's roughly 13 million more citizens who could invest in it if they chose to. This is bound to push the stocks up, and we may even see record highs in their value throughout the United States.

In fact, reports show that once Illinois made the move to legalize pot, sales soared through the roof. Within the first 12 days of legal operation, marijuana sales accrued approximately $20 million (Schuba, 2020). There was such a high demand for it that multiple stores had no choice but to start turning customers away on account of selling out so fast that they couldn't keep up.

This says a lot about the demand for legal marijuana. There is ample opportunity to make money because the market is not only standing strong, it's expanding. Other states are likely to follow suit in this, and we've witnessed this initial boom in sales before, when marijuana was legalized for recreational use in California.

Speaking of which, the United States is opening more of its doors to the legalization and trade of marijuana. With the significance of a midwestern state doing so, other states are likely to follow Illinois' lead. There are six states currently involved in motions to change marijuana legislation in favor of recreational use for adults: Arizona, Arkansas, Florida, Missouri, New Jersey and South Dakota (Williams, 2019). If these states were to join Illinois in succeeding this year, the climate for marijuana trading would change dramatically, and for the better.

Not to mention that with the legalization of marijuana in Illinois came another rectification that will benefit users, sellers and investors alike. State governor JB Pritzker included expungement in the state's new marijuana bill. Those previously convicted of carrying or using marijuana will have their records removed and charges lifted either automatically or with assistance from the courts depending on the severity of their arrest. Furthermore, the State of Illinois will also fund marijuana start-ups and focus on making it easier for convicted marijuana users to apply for business licenses.

There are also talks that authorities are starting to crack down on the illegal trade of marijuana. This has not been observed throughout the United States, but in California at least, law enforcement has warned peddlers that they're looking at hefty fines if they're caught (Romero, 2019). Though illicit dealing of marijuana has always been a punishable offense, it's being met with more urgency now that licenses are required to distribute pot. The illegal trade now has the power to damage legitimate businesses, and so state governments are taking a less forgiving stance.

It's even gone as far as to call out organizations that promote, or allow independent advertising of unlicensed dealers. We'll have to wait and see if the "guilty by association" approach assists in minimizing the illegal trade, but it seems promising.

Then, there's the big one—the national election that will take place later on in the year. Although marijuana trading is legal depending on state law, it's still considered a Schedule I drug— alongside heroin, LSD and MDMA.

Most people find it odd that marijuana is boxed in with some of the most destructive drugs in the world, but the system is not so simple. The problem is that a Schedule I drug is largely determined by two key traits:

- A lack of official health benefits or medical uses.
- High potential for abuse or addiction, be it psychological or physical.

Marijuana's classification as a Schedule I drug is based on how widespread it is. Since marijuana is by far the most popular drug (after alcohol), it makes sense that the government is on such high alert for it and has considered it one of the most dangerous of them all.

However, citizens don't agree with this decision and think it's silly that marijuana—a substance with few and mild negative impacts on society—is illegal, while alcohol and tobacco, two substances with undeniable destructive qualities, are not.

Recent polls show that the majority of Americans are calling for the total legalization of marijuana (Williams, 2020). One theory is that the new generation (Millennials) now has the most voting power and is slowly overruling older generations who still believe the stigma regarding the use of marijuana. Hence, the November 2020 election could swing in pot's favor.

President Trump has explicitly claimed that the federal government allows each state to decide for itself. He has also expressed support for the legal distribution of medical marijuana, and although he has not (as yet) made any progress is legalizing pot—medical or otherwise—on a federal level, no one can deny that he has followed through by giving states the go-ahead to write (or rewrite) their own marijuana laws. This is promising, and so long as he sticks to his resolve to let each state decide for itself, the country will be well on its way to total legalization.

In a similar vein, Bernie Sanders has pledged to legalize marijuana on his first day in the White House, should he be elected into it (Angell, 2020). We can't say for sure whether it's true, or big talk. Politicians have been observed to have a bark that is much bigger than their bite, but the reality remains that the current government—and its competition—are paying attention to what US citizens want. It serves as proof that marijuana is no longer demonized as it once was, and regardless of which side you align with, opinions regarding marijuana have become far more liberal.

We can also assume that the build-up to the election will emphasize the need to clean up the black market. Politicians are likely to put their best foot forward to gain the trust of voters. For the time being it is only an informed guess, but a highly probable one, logically speaking.

What Does This Mean for Pot Stocks?

The scene has been set. More states than we thought have reached legalization, while others are leaning closer toward it every day. Our government has realized that decriminalizing and commercializing marijuana will keep US citizens happy, and we live in an age when marijuana is no longer the Devil's lettuce and is now acknowledged as a mostly harmless recreational substance that adults should have the right to enjoy responsibly. This is bound to have a positive impact on pot stocks, but although it looks great in theory, what do the numbers say?

I'll be honest with you. People had little faith in pot stocks in 2019 because for a time the stocks' value plummeted. This was not because marijuana lost its worth, but rather the repercussion of shoddy planning and delays in service delivery. Canadian growers experienced a shortage of cannabis, US taxes were deemed too high to pay any attention to the pot stock market, and promises of supplementary products (like edibles, or e-joints) were left hanging. The demand for pot stocks didn't change, but unfortunately, the financial climate didn't accommodate or account for its value.

That said, by the end of 2019 things were looking up, and they seem to be on a steady ascent. Market growth was impressive in 2019, despite the bumps along the road and concerns that pot stocks weren't going anywhere.

Stats worth mentioning for 2019 include:

- Recreational sales increased by 48 percent, amounting to $8.9 billion in revenue.
- Medicinal marijuana sales increasing even more, at 54 percent, raking in $6.2 billion.
- The total spending on global marijuana sales reached 15 billion dollars.
- The USA accounted for 81 percent of total sales.
- Forecasts predict that 2020 will see further growth of at least 38 percent.

Contrary to all the concerns, the marijuana stock market did not falter as so many expected. It bounced back with a vengeance, paving the way for what we hope will be an excellent 2020 (Global Cannabis Sales Grow 48% to $15 Billion in 2019, 2020).

Taking everything into consideration; the legalization, expungement and aid in Illinois, presidential campaigns and discussions in the build-up to the election, booming sales for 2019 and more states looking to join the fun, things are looking good for pot stocks this year. It's one of the few times in US history that talks of total legalization and commercialization aren't being met with hostility. This has nurtured the market and planted the seeds for a much greener future.

Chapter 2:
Top 5 Marijuana Investing Mistakes and How to Avoid Them

An easy trap to fall into, is believing that because the market is strong, there is room for carelessness. As an investor—of anything, not just weed—it's all too easy to get ahead of yourself, or to become so confident that you trade irresponsibly, under the assumption that you can't go wrong.

If you're new to this, you have to understand that the stock market is extremely volatile. Traders learn by experience to predict which direction it will go in, to invest wisely and avoid losing money. Still, the market can slow, plummet or even crash at any given time.

It sounds like doom and gloom, or as though traders live in constant fear and paranoia, but the reality is that if you want to invest wisely you have to understand that there will always be a risk of choosing the wrong path.

Pot stocks are still relatively young compared to other facets of the stock market that we're accustomed to. This means that it carries its own risks and considerations outside of general trading. You want to apply the norms of trading to it still, but with a little extra caution, research, and awareness of what you're in for.

So, before we get into how you can trade marijuana and the best stocks to pay attention to, I want to show you what not to do. Bear in mind that this list is not exhaustive, but rather suggests the five most common and severe mistakes and how you can ensure that you don't make them.

#1. Putting All Your Eggs in One Basket

You may be tempted to concentrate all your efforts and money into one stock, but I must urge you not to give in to this. Diversification—the practice of keeping multiple stocks in your portfolio—is an essential concept in all trading, not just marijuana. The idea is that the more options you have, the less risk of loss you'll face.

To use an analogy, I'll take you back to the 2014 FIFA World Cup. Brazil, the team with the most world cup wins, based their entire strategy on one player in particular, Neymar, carrying them. He was hyped because he was their most popular (and some would argue skilled) player. He helped Brazil make it all the way to the semi-final, and then he got injured. When he was removed from play, and Brazil was left without their star,

Germany defeated them 7 goals to 1 (and then went on to win the entire tournament). If the Brazilian team had instead developed a strategy that wasn't Neymar-centric, they probably wouldn't have suffered such brutal obliteration when he couldn't play.

In trading, investing and finance it's much the same. If you have to invest all your money into one stock and that market crashes, you'll have lost everything. But, if you spread your funds over multiple stocks, you won't feel it as much if you lose one, and in fact, will stand a higher chance of garnering profits because you'll have various streams for it.

Though it applies to all trading, it is especially important to avoid this with marijuana. The market is still fresh, and therefore finding its feet. Backing only one horse with insufficient data to justify it could break you.

#2. Putting Your Eggs in Too Many Baskets

Following the first point, you must be careful not to do the inverse and opposite by investing in too many stocks. This is also an easy trap to fall into when you're just starting out, because the more avenues you have, the more secure you will feel. However, it's not a wise business decision as it could end up costing you more than it brings in returns.

If you have 30 stocks, chances are that the majority of them won't have much promise. Inevitably you'll spend money maintaining them in your portfolio that could be better spent on limited but more fruitful stocks. Your fees to keep low-performing stocks will add up over time, and it's likely that your returns won't break even with it. It's not worth it to waste money this way.

You'll also spread your investments too thin. The more stocks you invest in as a beginner, the smaller and less valuable those stocks will be. Sure, this reduces losses, but it also significantly decreases your potential payouts.

Managing countless stocks won't be fun, especially if you are inexperienced. It costs more, it demands more of your attention, and you'll have more to worry about. But you won't have more money. At least, it's rare that over diversifying works in the trader's favor.

Again, marijuana trading is no exception. Because the industry is still growing, there will be many, many duds in the market. It's okay to have good faith and try your luck, but ultimately if you try to invest in every marijuana stock, you will set yourself back.

#3. Guessing Instead of Researching

This applies to newbies and experienced traders. It's the stock market's nature to fluctuate, but this doesn't mean that traders "get lucky" when they invest in the right stocks. You're going to have to research pot stocks as a whole as much as you can before you put your money anywhere. Data can be analyzed to assess risk and predict gains, and there are other precautions you should take to set yourself up for a better chance of success.

Don't Only Buy What's Popular

Marijuana stocks are at a high risk of becoming over hyped as more states legalize it recreationally. There is a risk of inexperienced traders flooding the market and seemingly boosting new shares and stocks. It's likely that these will burn too bright too quickly, like with what happened to a company called Medmen. When it first joined the market, everybody had high hopes for it and expected it to dominate the industry. It started off with a huge bang and was well on track to living up to that expectation, keeping up with companies the likes of Apple— something previously unheard of in pot stocks.

But then, a string of unwise decisions and mismanagement caused Medmen to lose close to $200 million dollars in only four months. What added insult to injury is that Medmen raised enough money to cover their initial loss of $100 million, lost it, and then ended up in even hotter water (cnbc.com, 2019). As 2019 closed, analysts put Medmen on 'hold', meaning it's not advised to buy or sell any of its stocks at this time. Predictions also strongly suggest that Medmen is one of the few pot stocks that won't increase in value, or bring investors profits in 2020.

This isn't to say that you must absolutely avoid trending stocks. It's not always a bad idea to purchase them, but only on the condition that you have looked into the company, its projections and analyst predictions first. Don't just go by clout.

Don't Focus Too Much on Price

From the outside, it's easy to assume that the stock market is all about selling (or buying) price. I won't lie, it is critical and factors in immensely to a stock's success, but it's not what you should base your purchases on. Medmen is one example. Its stocks initially went for $2 each, but it's abundantly clear that spending those two dollars wasn't a smart idea. That's where market capitalization comes in.

To put it simply, a company's market cap is the total value of a company's outstanding shares. The calculation is simple. Multiply the price of the shares by the number of shares. So, if a company had one million outstanding shares selling at $1 dollar each, the company's market cap is one million dollars. This is a much better gauge of a company's potential, and it should definitely be considered in your decision to invest.

Another thing you need to pay attention to is a company's dilution. If it has too many stocks, or if its stocks are expanding at a ridiculous rate, the value of its shares will decrease. It's inevitable that when a company first starts out there will be some initial dilution, but if it doesn't stabilize, it's a massive red flag.

These are just a few examples of stats and facts that you should look into before investing. You're at full liberty to purchase stocks that are affordable or widespread and hope for the best because as I mentioned the market fluctuates and anything could happen. You very well could strike lucky. However, if you are looking to nurture gains, you must not view trading as gambling. You win some, you lose some, yes. But unlike a game of poker, you can see the cards that companies can play. Base your buying decision on analysis, not guesswork, and you'll remove many risks when settling.

#4. Don't Jump the Gun

Regardless of what I've mentioned above, the marijuana market is still finding its feet so current trends in it are somewhat unstable because it hasn't had enough time to plant its flag into the ground. As stated in the introduction, forecasts predict that in the next six years, marijuana stocks will rake in more than $150 billion. It's not to say that the low performing shares now will still be such then, and it's not to say that the high-value shares of 2020 will stand firm by the end of the decade.

This applies to all trading , of course, but it's more of a risk when speaking specifically of marijuana. As more states legalize, that inevitable boom will occur and stock values will experience an initial peak. It's entirely up to you when you want to sell your shares, but you must understand that hanging on to them may be more fruitful in the future.

There's a popular non-marijuana related example of why timing is everything. It's difficult to believe now, but back in the 1990s, Google was secondary to the dominating internet force of the time - Yahoo. In 1998, Google co-founders Larry Page and Sergey Brin offered to sell Google's page rank system to Yahoo for a measly $1 million, but Yahoo refused, choosing to build its own empire instead. In 2003, Google approached Yahoo again, this time looking to sell its rising service for $3 million dollars, but Yahoo stuck to its guns and once more declined, planning to develop its own search engine that would knock Google out of the park (Akolowala, 2016).

It failed. Miserably. Now, Google is synonymous with the internet as a whole, while Yahoo barely exists anymore.

In trading, you can't think too much on the "what-ifs", because if you do you will be compelled to invest in everything, and as I said that's a mistake. You have to pick your corners wisely, and will inevitably reject or cut stocks that may have been a good idea to buy and keep. You can't kick yourself too hard, but in Yahoo's case, it's something the company will never recover from. If it had purchased Google back in 1998, when it was worth a lot less than it is now, there's a good chance that the company wouldn't have fallen into the background. Google was handed to it on a silver platter, but it "wasn't good enough" and turning it away led to Yahoo's own near-demise.

Remember this in trading pot stocks, as it ties directly into not only buying what's popular or what looks like it will be a winner. Timing is essential while the market grows, and it's worth it to refrain from counting your chickens before they hatch.

#5. Buying in Based on Hype

Everyone wants a piece of the pot stocks pie, and because of new regulations and motions to legalize it, there are many people that assume that investing in marijuana now is the fastest and easiest way to make a big buck. That, or they just want bragging rights in the "420" community.

However, because pot stocks have only recently entered the stock market, its economy is somewhat unpredictable. While it's as safe as any other trade, there are countless factors that are working against it and that could swing either way in the future. One is supply and demand. The industry has mostly relied on Canadian suppliers, but it's looking like there isn't enough to go around. Companies have raised capital to meet the demand, but the economy could take a turn for the worst at any given moment, and that could mean that resources for the marijuana market could plummet, or even crash completely.

It's not to deter you from investing. The climate is doing well, and as explained, it's expected to grow exponentially in the next few years. But if you're not a serious investor, or you are only interested in this as a gimmick, you could over saturate the market and therefore cause values to drop, or lose out from putting too much faith in this fairly new industry. This also ties into doing your research.

Make sure that marijuana stocks are something you are genuinely interested in investing in for business's sake. Learn all you can about where and when to invest your money, and make an effort to understand the economy as it is now, and the potential risks of investing in it.

Another thing you shouldn't do is investing in the sale of the weed itself just because you can. Marijuana stocks span various industries, and it could be that investing in its real estate, distribution, ancillary or other connected products and services is a wiser decision than investing in its cultivation. It's worth looking into, because the marijuana itself isn't actually the be-all and end-all of the pot industry.

Choose Wisely

If anything, the takeaway for this chapter should be to choose your investments wisely. More advice I can give you is to look into all the regulations so that you can have a better understanding of where the market is headed.

It's understandable that there are so many eager investors who want in on this exciting opportunity, but you have to keep in mind that the novelty will eventually wear off. This will affect the market for it, and that will affect you.

Remember that this isn't drug dealing, it's trading. If you don't approach pot stocks as a trader, I'm sorry to say, you likely won't get very far in this endeavor.

Chapter 3: Risks in Investing in Marijuana Stocks

Even though we've covered what not to do, there is no guarantee that you will be successful in your marijuana trading. This is not because it's marijuana, but rather because by nature, trading is a bit of a risky business. All the considerations attached to trading as a whole apply to pot stocks, but of course there are some that are industry specific.

Many people have been blinded by the charm of marijuana entering the stock market. It's great that it's been so well-received, but just because it's weed, it doesn't mean it's worth losing money over.

So, again, before we get to the fun part (discussing which stocks you *should* buy), let's take a look at the potential perils of buying and selling pot stocks. Pay attention to these. They could be the difference between a successful venture or a mistake you can't recover from. You don't want to be the next Medmen or Yahoo, do you?

Laws May Affect Trading

Let's start with the most obvious and pressing one. All the projections, forecasts, and predictions for pot stocks are based on the fact that marijuana companies have the freedom to operate in the stock market. Things are looking good because of all the favorable laws and regulations being passed, but it would be silly to assume that this is how it will remain.

It's unlikely that the government will change its mind about legalization or go back on new decriminalization laws, but the problem is that all of these laws are state only. Federal law still has marijuana listed alongside heroin as a Schedule I drug, and if the federal government decides to overrule every single state it's been allowed in, there'll be nothing that traders can do. It's improbable, but still possible. This also means that even if distributing marijuana is legal in your state, you're still vulnerable to federal prosecution.

Even without federal interference, laws can still work against pot stocks. It's likely that as marijuana trading grows in popularity, new regulation will be implemented to control tax, distribution, licensing, real estate and all other facets of it. If the current businesses aren't prepared for the cracking of these whips, they may falter and go under.

The black market is also a concern, as it not only dampens the legal sale of it by making it more affordable than it should be, but laws to combat it could affect business. Stricter rules, in an effort to restrict illegal trading of marijuana, is inevitable. This will impact distribution as well as supply and demand which has a direct effect on the stock market.

It Might Not Pan Out

Remember that all the projections for pot stocks might not come to be. The estimates and forecasts are as accurate as is possible, but they're not a matter of fact. It's wise to follow the thought of "expecting the best but preparing for the worst" (or the other way around if you're a pessimist). Come 2025, the marijuana market may disappoint us all or even disappear off the radar. Even if it's here to stay, there's also the possibility that returns may not be as high as you hope they will be. Some people are even of the opinion that the current climate is its peak and that from here on out, it can only continue in a straight line or drop. In all areas of trading, there is the possibility that the experts and analysts are wrong.

The marijuana-specific problem here is that all the projections are based on an industry that's so new, evaluation of profits, risks, and stability are incredibly difficult to do. Marijuana needs more time in the stock market before our analyses can be taken as gold.

I realize that in the previous chapter, I explicitly told you not to guess, and to do your research first. This still stands. The word of the experts still matters and still has value, but it's not the only thing you should go by. You must account for the economic climate of marijuana as well, and there's no denying that it is a bit untidy as it stands now.

Understand that regardless of whether experts have come to expect high returns, the market is volatile because of all the external factors that have to be accounted for. At the end of the day, recreational marijuana is still illicit in most of the world, and most states too. Just because it looks like society is opening up to it, it doesn't mean that it will. Even if it does, there's a chance that it will take much longer to be decriminalized than you hope.

Commoditization

This one is fascinating but no less risky. One of the most important reasons why marijuana stocks are looking so good is because... well... it's marijuana. It stands out, it appeals to people who ordinarily wouldn't consider investing or trading and there is a ridiculously massive market for it. Commoditization could ruin that.

This occurs when a commodity loses its power, is grouped in with the rest and becomes indistinguishable from others therefore its value (and appeal) on the stock market is significantly diminished. Marijuana will always be a commodity, but technically so are carrots. When last did you see carrots making economic headlines? A carrot is a carrot, and they only have value when unforeseen circumstances (like droughts) kick in and the demand sorely outweighs the supply.

Commoditization can also be defined as the occurrence of a price being the only difference between similar products. Brands will then be in direct competition with each other and lose control over their own prices in fear of chasing customers away to more affordable alternatives. For example, if, on average, one bottle of water costs $1, it doesn't matter if one brand with a nicer bottle sells it for $1.50. The mark-up is almost insignificant, and most people won't accuse the company of being dirty thieves. If however, they charge 15 dollars for that same bottle, few people would bother buying it. It's water, and you could buy a product of equal quality for 14 dollars less.

As marijuana sales boom, competition is likely to spark and suppliers will have to find ways to keep up with each other. Weed may not be as simple as water (and don't forget that it's not just the plant, but its accessories and real estate too), but the more popular it becomes, the higher the risk of devaluing it.

Dilution

I've already touched on this, but it's in line with the previous point. Marijuana has huge potential to turn entirely mainstream. This isn't a future threat, it's possible right now because of the dilution of shares.

As companies attempt to break into the market, they will sell more shares and stocks at a lower price, in an effort to reach more people. This could swing either way. Maybe it will serve the stocks well, or maybe it will turn them into toilet paper.

Aurora Cannabis is the best (or worst?) example of this. This particular company was one of the leading forces in the market, branching into both retail and wholesale, and spreading further than any other marijuana company thought it could. Now, it's facing bankruptcy because it tried to do too much, with too little resource and ended up diluting its own stocks to its own detriment. When Aurora Cannabis started out, it had approximately 16 million shares. Now, it has more than a billion shares and is struggling to keep itself afloat.

Instances of this may be few and far between, but there is an increased risk for pot stocks because of desperate new companies trying to claim their stock market ground. There is definitely a market that will buy into this because new traders often assume that cheap is better.

It goes hand in hand with commoditization. Too much interest is a bad thing in trading. The more there is of something, the less value it has.

Financial Backing May Be Scarce

This problem only affects the USA currently because of our odd system of having federal laws separate from state laws. The problem is that banks and other financial services must abide by federal law, and so, many of them are unwilling to support marijuana businesses regardless of state legality.

If you're looking to sell stocks or set up your own marijuana business it goes without saying that this presents a bit of an unfair obstacle. Loans and insurance are largely out of the question, and this affects buyers as well.

Marijuana companies are forced to operate independently and so, don't have the security of other companies or industries in the stock market. If anything were to happen to these companies, that means that you, the customer, won't be protected either. It also means that many marijuana businesses prefer to do business in person, with physical cash exchanging hands. It can slow the progression of marijuana business as capital will be more difficult to raise too.

Are the Risks Worth It?

If traders were deterred at the first sign of trouble, the stock market wouldn't exist. These risks aren't in any way an implication that pot stocks aren't worth it, but rather a warning that investing might not be as easy or simple as you'd originally thought. There are many considerations, both legal and financial when it comes to trading, but that's just it. It's trading. No stocks are 100 percent safe from collapse.

The best thing you can do to protect yourself is to understand what you're getting yourself into in trading marijuana. I'd very much like to tell you that there are simple solutions to each of these problems, but the harsh reality is that there aren't any. Not because the market is a bad one to consider, but because each issue is beyond your control as a buyer.

So, what you should do is what I've already advised. Do your research, pay attention to the market, and base your decisions on information rather than sentiment, excitement or luck. Trade responsibly and you'll be just fine.

The key is to weigh up your options and figure out which investments and practices are worth it to you. So, now that we've got the obligatory safety demonstration out of the way, you can bucklc up and prepare for take-off.

Chapter 4:
These Two Marijuana Stocks Could Be the Biggest Winners in 2020

It seems that marijuana investors haven't learned to dig a little deeper. This could be because the industry has its leading lights that are blinding us to the rest (Aurora Cannabis, Medmen, and CanopyGrowth to name three). It may also be the reason why analysts, advisors and some forecasters lost faith in the market. They zoomed in on terrible examples of what pot stocks can be, and the entire industry took the fall for it.

But, as I said, the market bounced back and interest is once again blossoming. There are two stocks in particular that I feel are underrated and overlooked when it comes to investing. Note that the following should not be taken as ultimate advice to buy into them. I do feel that regardless, you should keep an eye on them because of their potential and promising stats.

Planet 13 Holdings Inc

(OTCMKTS:PLNHF, CNSX:PLTH).

Planet 13 Holdings deals with the cultivation, preparation, and distribution of marijuana. Currently, it owns the largest marijuana dispensary in the world—the Planet 13 Cannabis Entertainment Complex, near the Las Vegas strip. The store operates all day, every day and deals with the company's selection of products, varying from edibles to vapes, pre-rolled cannabis cigarettes, concentrates, merchandise and more. The complex has proven itself to be highly successful with more than 3000 visitors a day, and average annual consumer expenditure sitting at just under $95—an 8.4 percent increase between years. This single complex also accounts for nearly 10 percent of Nevada's marijuana sales, and the way things are looking, this percentage is likely to inflate in the coming years. Projects in the work for Planet 13 Holdings include a dispensary in California, a restaurant in Las Vegas, and a warehouse for production in its home town too.

Why It's Worth Watching

Planet 13 Holdings had a good year in 2019 and finished strong (Inc, 2019). Reports show that at the end of the third quarter of 2019, the company's revenue had grown by 241 percent. The stats from 2019 include:

- Revenue of $16.7 million.
- A net loss of $1.7 million (up from $0.9 million the previous year).
- Net income of $30,000 (before tax).
- The company has adjusted its earnings before interest, tax, depreciation and amortization (EBITDA) to $3.4 million (compared to $376,611 in 2018).
- A reported $18.1 million of capital.

Analysts, forecasts, and predictions imply that 2020 will be an even better year for Planet 13 Holdings as creases are ironed out and the company continues to advance. The stock has risen 77% in the last year, and forecasts predict that by the end of 2020 stock will be valued at

$3.95, almost double what it is now ($2). Some predictions suspect that this spike will be much higher, and that Planet 13 Holdings stock could rise as high as $4.25, a 113 percent increase.

GrowGeneration Corp

(NASDAQ:GRWG)

This company owns the largest hydroponic and organic marijuana gardening centers in the country. It has an online division, and caters to customers who grow their own marijuana, supplying equipment, nutrient, soil, and other tools to both individuals and commercial growers. Currently, there are 26 such stores scattered across Colorado (the company's home ground), California, Washington, Michigan, Maine, Nevada, Oklahoma, Rhode Island, and New Hampshire.

Current expansions and ongoing projects include the purchase of GrowWorld in 2019, taking over the Portland company's assets and operations in hydroponics. It may not sound as spectacular as Planet 13 Holdings, but its numbers are even better.

Why It's Worth Watching

GrowGeneration broke records in 2019 (GrowGeneration, 2019). Revenue reports show that the company advanced by 159 percent year-to-year, ending off 2019's third quarter with $21.8 million. The company also reported:

- Net income of $1 million.
- Adjusted EBITDA of $2 million (a significant difference compared to $71,584 in the third quarter of 2018).
- $16 million capital in cash and cash equivalents.

The company is kicked off 2020 trading shares at approximately $4.14, a 75 percent year-to-year increase. Predictions expect this to go up even further, with forecasts suggesting that stocks will end 2020 at anywhere between $8 and $9.50, increasing more than 100 percent.

Which Should You Pick?

At first glance, it may seem like Planet 13 Holdings is where it's at because of its expansion, capital and impressive improvements since 2019. All of this is true, but GrowGeneration (fitting to its name) grew exponentially and more steadily than the former and is predicted to have more valuable stocks by the end of the year.

Ultimately, both of these should be on your watch list, as they're two of the most promising pot stocks for new and seasoned investors alike.

Chapter 5:
Two Pot Stocks You Should Avoid in 2020

Determining where to put your money is one thing. Figuring out which stocks to avoid like the plague is an entirely different story. That buyer bias I mentioned earlier factors in a lot here. Assuming that stocks are cheap, and are therefore easy to make money with is one rookie mistake. Believing a company to be a good choice based on popularity alone is another. Sometimes, reading too much into a company's glory days while ignoring their deteriorating track record is the biggest problem.

It's not easy to cut your losses, but sometimes you have to admit that investing, or continuing to invest in certain stocks is a big mistake that will come back to bite you.

The recession felt across the entire industry in 2019 knocked quite a few businesses over. While some managed to dust themselves off, others just simply couldn't recover. Two stocks in particular are not showing healthy signs for investing. The funny (or sad) thing about this is that they're the only two stocks that Wall Street is warning against this year, even though they were by far the most popular in previous years. Let's take a look at them now.

CanopyGrowth

(NYSE:CGC)

The truly depressing reality about CanopyGrowth is that it began with all the potential in the world. In fact, it was the first cannabis company in North America to join the stock market. Its premise—not just selling marijuana products, but developing them for the mainstream—left it in good standing with advocates across the continent. It was well on its way to total domination of the industry, with all boxes checked. Perceived to be one of the leaders in weed production around the world, everyone believed that CanopyGrowth was it. The company's records tell a much different story, and it seems that the cracks can't be filled (Corporation, 2019). The numbers are thus:

- C$76.6 million in net sales, dropping 15 percent from the previous quarter.

- C$265.8 million in operating losses, weighed down even more by a further C$389 million loss (also operations-based) in the first six months of the new fiscal year.

The company's records and balance sheets continue to worsen, due largely in part to irresponsible spending by the company. Regardless of its losses, it insists on expanding, even going as far as to overpay for assets that it already can't afford. Word is that CanopyGrowth's goodwill (intangible assets, like acquired brands and trademarks) has inflated to C$1.91 billion, cutting a massive chunk out of its only saving grace, Constellation Brands' $4 billion dollar investment.

It's no wonder then that CanopyGrowth stocks are expected to depreciate. It seems as though the company thought it could get by on clout alone and got way too far ahead of itself. Rather than rethinking its strategy, it's trying to stay on top, not realizing that it is snowballing into disaster in its stubbornness.

For these reasons, CanopyGrowth is unanimously one of the pot stocks that you shouldn't even consider in 2020, lest you be dragged down with it. Its value declined by close to 10 percent in January alone.

CronosGroup
(NASDAQ:CRON)

If reading about CanopyGrowth left a sour taste in your mouth, CronosGroup won't be a palette cleanser. Performing even worse than the former, this company has a current downside of 16.8 percent (nearly twice as much as CanopyGrowth). It's another example of how a brand's first impressions could be a false indicator of a company's value. CronosGroup ended the year off with C$2 billion in cash and cash equivalents and is ranked number 2, after CanopyGrowth for cash on hand.

To the untrained eye, CronosGroup seems like the perfect business venture, but as with the previous example, not all that glitters is gold.

For one, CronosGroup just isn't keeping up with other companies of its scale, type, and niche. Though the brand grows marijuana, it's producing 40 percent of the goods of its competitors. While it's headed for expansion later in 2020 the fact remains that its market cap is nowhere near as high as it should (or could) be.

The second problem is that CronosGroup, like CanopyGrowth, just doesn't know when to stop. Even though the company brought in C$12.7 million in net sales, its production costs and operating expenses are costing the company almost quadruple that.

Lastly, CronosGroup has some PR resuscitation to do. The company manufactures as distributes marijuana vapes, but new evidence has linked the use of such to severe, and even deadly lung disease. Sure, CronosGroup isn't responsible or liable for this, but people are pulling away from these products, and warning others to do the same.

In a similar fashion to CanopyGrowth, CronosGroup simply isn't doing well and seemingly making no real effort to right its wrongs. With the same stubbornness, it is reaching too high and is bound to topple offer if it doesn't steady itself.

What If You Choose to Invest Anyway?

Well, nothing is stopping you from throwing your money away if you really want to, but it's not recommended.

To clarify, it's not to say that CanopyGrowth and CronosGroup will never, ever recover. Perhaps they'll bounce back in the future, and be worth your investment at a later time, but not now and the way it's looking, not for a while.

It's unwise to invest in them in 2020, based on their declining worth and irresponsible business decisions. There are countless promising stocks to consider, and unfortunately, these two just don't make the cut.

Chapter 6:
15 High Potential Marijuana Stocks that Could Make You Rich Quick

I know that I have emphasized that you shouldn't look at pot stocks as an effortless way of making money. You're going to have to put some thought and planning into it, and don't forget that you will have to pay for the stocks that you are interested in. Don't invest in any and all pot stocks that you come across. Sure, you might hit the jackpot if you do, but if it were that easy, trading wouldn't be considered a skill. It's better to look into each stock and company so that you can make an informed decision and capitalize on your earnings.

That said, just because trading isn't mindless or free of administration and labor, it doesn't mean that you can't make a lot of money in a relatively short amount of time. That's what trading is all about. Sure, you can look at it as a way to maximize your income over time, but with the right knowledge you could cash in easily without committing to a lifetime of trading. It all depends on what you're after.

I must disclaim that regardless of what is listed in this chapter, you are the only person who is responsible for your trading decisions. I'm in no way telling you to invest in these stocks if you don't want to, nor am I guaranteeing that they will prove fruitful.

My recommendations are based on the stocks that are heading in the right direction and that is likely to continue on an upward path. However, remember that stocks fluctuate and that by the time you read this, their potential may have changed.

I'd also like to remind you that you can invest in multiple stocks, but to keep in mind that you shouldn't go after all of them. There are 25 stocks listed here. Most experts believe that you should aim to spread your investments over no more than 20 stocks in your portfolio. Keep in mind that this number generally speaks of seasoned investors and traders, and may be excessive and stressful for beginners in the industry. If that's the case, choose as many as you are comfortable with, but I would recommend taking on 10 or less when starting out.

Think of this as a starting square. The steps that you take from here on out are entirely up to you.

If You Want to Play it Safe:

Curleaf Industries (CURLF)

To start off, Curleaf Industries is on investor watch lists because it bounced right back from the concerning recession that affected all pot stocks. Reports from November 2019 show that these stocks are on a steady rise, increasing in value by at least 35 percent—impressive, considering the roller coaster that all pot stocks went through in 2018. It's impossible to say for sure whether these stocks will continue to grow, but by the look of it, nothing is standing in the way. The company has made some sound business decisions, though, like acquiring GR Companies (Grassroots), which has allowed it to broaden its horizons and expand its dispensaries.

Innovative Industrial Properties (IIPR)

Though this one doesn't deal directly with the pot itself it is undoubtedly one of the best investments you can make in this industry. Innovative Industrial Properties deals with real estate. More specifically it's a real estate investment trust (REIT), something rare in the marijuana world. What this means is that it buys and then leases properties suitable for the production, dispensing, sale and distribution of marijuana products.

Innovative Industrial Properties was the first marijuana company to be listed on the major and mainstream stock exchange. It was also one of the few that wasn't affected by the recession, and to the contrary, rose in value when all the others were plummeting. In 2018 stocks grew by 39 percent. In 2019, it knocked most others out of the park by increasing a further 72 percent.

As more states legalize marijuana, it's likely that Innovative Industrial Properties will expand and increase in worth even more.

cbdMD (YBD)

Based in North Carolina, investors are eager to see which road these stocks travel down (or up, rather). One belief is that because it's an all-American company, it's rapport, customer service and reputation works in its favor. It has also created job opportunities for American citizens, and so there is a sense of loyalty surrounding it. But of course, trading and patriotism are two different things.

Though cbdMD doesn't have as high numbers as the two previously listed stocks, it has the highest potential of all of them. Its portfolio is extremely diverse, dealing in oils, edibles, and equipment. Its biggest trump is that the CBD it deals is non-psychoactive and so its market is much wider.

Projections assume that in the coming years CBD will grow to a billion-dollar industry, and since cbdMD is already dominating, it's likely to benefit.

Truelieve Cannabis (TCNFF)

Following the previous entry, here is another that doesn't focus on getting high, but rather on helping those in need. Truleive Cannabis not only provides medical marijuana, but it also makes an effort to develop it further and advises on the subject.

2018 wasn't a fantastic year for these stocks, but Truelieve recovered well and is now one of the few that has kept criticism at bay. It may not boast exciting numbers like others on this list, but it's not operating at a loss and has kept its numbers consistent, regardless of the lull two years ago.

GW Pharmaceuticals (GWPH)

Representatives of GW Pharmaceuticals have explicitly expressed a desire to distance the company from other pot stocks, but there is no doubt that it's one of the safest bets you can make. As of January 2020, its market cap is the second highest of them all. GW Pharmaceuticals is another example of how most marijuana-based stocks took a knock in the aftermath of the recession, but its CBD-based drug, Epidiolex, pulled it right out of its rut.

It's been on a steady incline since then and is one of the stocks predicted to remain persistently profitable well into the future.

Honorable Mention: iAnthus Capital Holdings (CNSX)

In January 2020 iAnthus ranked as both one of the best value pot stocks and one of the fastest-growing stocks. At the time, stocks were available for as little as CA$1.96, while its market cap was CA$336.3. This presents little opportunity for risk, and since it is on a fast growth track is well worth paying attention to.

The Canadian company boasts CBD For Life and Grow Healthy Holdings as subsidiaries, and deals with the production, distribution and dispensing of marijuana products throughout the USA.

Medium-Risk Pot Stocks:

Harvest Health and Recreation (HRVSF)

It may not be as well known as other pot stocks but it's certainly on the rise. HRVSF is one of the largest stocks that you can invest in, with a total of 210 marijuana licenses under its belt. It operates in 18 states and has garnered quite a large following in Arizona, one of the most likely states to legalize recreational marijuana in 2020.

Currently, Harvest Health's market cap is sitting at $930 million. It's considered a medium risk pot stock because some investors are uncertain when it comes to its consistency, with drops in shares recorded in the recession. However, it's featuring on lists on pot stocks to watch and may be well on its way to reclaiming its billion-dollar status by the end of the year.

Green Thumb Industries (GTBIF)

Green Thumb Industries isn't risky, it's just that it needs more time to prove itself before it joins the ranks of others like Truelieve, Gw Pharmaceuticals or Innovative Properties. It's the talk of the town though, and there's no time like the present to invest in it.

Green Thumb currently has 34 retail stores, 96 retail licenses and operates across 12 states. Its potential for high returns is on the rise because of

Illinois's move to legalize marijuana and joining the ranks of Green Thumb's widespread market (estimated to be as many as 151 million people).

The company is rumored to be in the process of opening 10 new stores in Illinois, and this is bound to boost its stocks in the next few years.

Aphria (APHA)

Aphria's reputation might precede it, but some light needs to be shed on the situation. In December 2018, accusations of fraud surfaced and in the chaos, backlash, and aftermath of the recession, the then CEO stepped down. This meant that Aphria had to spend 2019 doing damage control, and many people lost faith that the company was worth investing in.

It proved everyone wrong, as its stocks are on the rise again, and doing a good job of maintaining their stability. This is largely thanks to Aphria's acquisition of CC Pharma. It's also worth noting that Aphria is Canada's third-largest grower.

As it turns out, the allegations made against the company were untrue. The problem is that some people may not trust the brand anymore, and this could impact their stocks in the future.

Sprott Inc. (SII)

Sprott Inc. is actually doing really well on the stock market, so it may not be entirely fair to list it as a medium-risk investment. However, it just acquired Tocqueville Asset Management LP for a considered $50 million, on condition that the acquisition fulfills desired financial goals over the next two years.

This decision has given Sprott Inc huge momentum, but we'll have to see how it plays out before we can say with certainty that Sprott is worth backing.

Sprott Inc is an asset management company, that assists clients with investment and portfolio management, mediation between client and broker, and consultations. It's not a true marijuana business but is one of the few that doesn't discriminate against cannabis companies, so I feel it's worth a mention.

The Valens Co. (VLNS)

This Canadian company processes and develops marijuana. Like Sprott Inc. it's doing extremely well on the market, is growing perfectly and has gained a lot of momentum moving forward, but because of recent expansions, we'll have to give it time.

The Valens Co. acquired Pommies Cider Co. in November 2019, under similar conditions to what was mentioned above. The company has plans to branch out into Eastern Canada, and this is apparently the first step.

It's looking good, and the Valens Co. is likely to be a great investment, but there is still a risk that their decisions might not work out.

High-Risk, High-Gain Stocks:

Before I list the high-risk stocks, I want to warn you that I don't personally recommend these to beginner traders. There is a lot of money to be made in these, but it can be extremely difficult to gauge when to sell your stocks with high-risk companies. That said, I am not telling you what to do, and if you are feeling up to the challenge, I won't stop you from buying into these. Just know what you're getting into.

Another note I'd like to add is that there is a difference between high-risk, high-gain stocks, and write-offs. Earlier I mentioned that two in particular, CanopyGrowth and CronosGroup, should be avoided. This is because they aren't showing any signs of recovery or growth and the risk of loss far outweighs the potential for any gains.

For this reason, I will exclude them from this list. Others that are seemingly popular, but not recommended include Aurora Cannabis and Tilray.

Emerald Health Therapeutics (EMHTF)

This company grows marijuana and has expanded faster than most others in the industry. In 2018, it partnered with Village Farms International to include marijuana in their production. It was an excellent decision that saved large amounts of money and effort on Emerald Health's part. Emerald Health then went on to invest in its own 1 million square feet growing space.

It's one of the largest growers in Canada, but there are two problems. One is that this company stands the risk of oversupply. The second is that stocks are a bit low currently, likely from the recession that affected all marijuana businesses.

There is still potential for Emerald Health Therapeutics to make a comeback, and if the election works in our favor later this year, it could swing in this company's favor.

Acreage Holdings (ACRGF)

This is a bit of an odd one. This company deals with production, processing and dispensing, and has made a name for itself in the legal battle for marijuana.

On one account, there aren't any complaints that target Acreage Holdings that don't apply to other business (for example, the recession being a factor in dropping stocks). On the other hand, the climate is recovering from the recession and Acreage Holdings, like many others, could make a comeback if it plays its cards right. The problem has nothing to do with its stocks, though.

Acreage Holdings has a deal with CanopyGrowth, which as I explained is not one that you want to invest in right now. The terms are that the latter will acquire Acreage Holdings for $34 billion, but only if marijuana is legalized in the United States.

It may be a good choice to invest in Acreage and hope that it gets back on its feet, but 2020 could very well be the year that the federal government changes marijuana's classification. If this happens, the deal with CanopyGrowth will come to pass. I don't have to explain why this is a huge risk.

Hexo (HEXO)

Hexo's strategies are excellent. It has a long-term plan in place, and many people believe that this company will go on to great things. However, its numbers are disappointing and stockholders have been on a roller coaster until now.

Some analysts say that Hexo is unlikely to recover from its losses in 2019. Others believe that its partnership with Molson Coors Brewing is its saving grace.

Marijuana products like drinks and edibles are on the rise, and it could be that Hexo had the foresight to buy into the industry before it boomed. It is risky to invest in Hexo stocks, but you never know. It might pay off more than any other on this list.

MariMed (MRMD)

MariMed is another marijuana real estate company. The truth is that its 2019 reports were absolute garbage. It was one of the worst performers in the industry, and its shares dropped by 81 percent.

It's one of the riskiest to invest in right now, but it has a few traits that keep people interested. For one, it owns 300,000 square feet of space for growing and production. For another, it may be slow on the rise, but by the look of it, it's over the worst.

Again, the election could change everything for these stocks. If marijuana is legalized, real estate for it will boom. 2020 could be the year that MariMed re-enters the game, and even dominates it.

A Word of Warning

The stocks that I have listed above are the ones that seem promising, but remember that the stock market changes regularly. In all cases (the low risk as well as the high risk ones) their numbers, stats and standings are not set in stone. That is the nature of investing and trading, so if you choose to buy into any of them, proceed with caution and do so at your own risk.

Chapter 7:
What Investors Need to Know About Marijuana Real Estate

You've had a good look at which stocks are doing well, so let's take a break from the numbers for a bit and focus on the other facets of the marijuana industry. It's safe to assume that outside of production and distribution of the marijuana itself, real estate for it is the next point of interest.

However, remember that what is popular isn't always good and won't guarantee a fruitful investment. Marijuana real estate is a good example of this, because, as much as there is massive potential to earn money with it, it's just as risky as trading shares, if not riskier.

So, before you continue with this chapter, keep in mind that all the dos and don'ts still apply. Investing in marijuana real estate shouldn't be seen as a way to bypass the instability of investing in companies or brands. You should still do as much research as possible before you jump in, and will do well to approach this as you would any other business venture.

What is Marijuana Real Estate?

Marijuana real estate is simply the property that marijuana businesses operate from. This could be a store from which medicinal marijuana is dispensed, a plot of land where it's organically cultivated, hydroponic growing facilities, or factories in which ancillary products are manufactured.

Now that marijuana is legalized in some states, there is no need to produce or use it in secret. It's possible to set up shop (no matter what trade you are in), without the suspicious stares from the neighbors and fear of police raids.

At least, that's what people think but it's a little bit more complicated than that. You may be able to trade pot stocks willy nilly through the stock market, but if you are supplying real estate for it, chances are you're going to need a license to do that.

It's not because the government is being spiteful, it's merely common sense. Marijuana is produced for public consumption and therefore has to meet health and safety regulation. You can set up a dispensary as easily as you can a brewery. It's only fair.

This raises some complications for everyone concerned, because it raises the question of whether or not marijuana real estate truly is legal.

We've gone over how on a federal-level marijuana is still entirely illegal. Part of the deal in the "each to their own" approach when it comes to state law, is that your state will regulate your business. While it's one thing to trade marijuana, even though it's technically still illegal, it's a whole different game when it comes to supply and distribution. It opens up a whole can of worms.

Laws You Should Be Aware Of

So, you may be thinking that because federal law isn't enforced, there's no harm in living and letting live, and investing in marijuana real estate anyway. There's a low probability that you will get into trouble for it, and if your state allows trading, you're good to go, right?

Not quite. The more you look into marijuana real estate, the more you'll see why you may want to reconsider investing in it, especially if you're new to this. Here's what you should know when it comes to federal law:

- The use, sale, distribution and production of marijuana is entirely illegal regardless of the state you are in. Thus, if you are dispensing, growing or trading it, you are still in violation of the law.

- The Controlled Substances Act implies that even if you are not directly involved with marijuana businesses, you may still be guilty of profiting from drug trafficking by association. This is important, because if you were to lease property to someone else who then uses your land or space to grow marijuana, you are just as responsible as your tenants, even if you have no part in their business.

- This means that under federal law, you can be fired, evicted, denied your right to bear arms, and denied service from institutions like banks because of this association to federal crimes in doing business with you.

- By the same token, if you invest in any marijuana real estate, you will be committing a federal crime.

- Even worse, you can still face federal charges from simply holding or using marijuana without the intention of selling, distributing or producing it.

- Penalties for committing such crimes depend on the offense, but are known to range from fines (anywhere between $1000 and $1 million), to prison time.

What Does This Mean for Investors?

You can still go ahead and buy into marijuana real estate, but you must consider the implications of how federal law governs it. It may be acceptable and appropriate for real estate businesses to set up shop in the states they're in, but there is always the threat of persecution looming in the background. Beyond this:

- Real estate businesses may experience difficulty in expansion, funding or even promotion, due to the associations with federal law violation.

- For the same reason, it's tricky for marijuana real estate owners to acquire the necessary paperwork beyond funding and title deeds. Insurance is a big one, as few companies are willing to provide this service considering the overall restriction and possibility of prosecution.

- If you are investing in or managing a property yourself, be aware that there are many regulations in terms of the location and systems and processes of the facility. For example, many states impose limits. It's not uncommon for regulation to dictate that your facility must be at least 100 feet outside of residential areas, and 1000 feet away from schools, playgrounds, libraries or other spots likely to attract children, for example. If you or your chosen business does not abide by these restrictions, it may be subject to persecution on a state level. The same applies to health and safety laws.

- One survey found that residential areas in close proximity to dispensaries saw significant decreases in overall property value (*Marijuana and Real Estate: A Budding Issue*, 2020).

- Common complaints reported with regard to marijuana facilities are unpleasant smells, property damage by fire or damp, and theft.

But it's not all difficult. Despite these restrictions and complications, marijuana real estate is still growing as an industry, with more people investing it and an increase in demand for marijuana facilities, with reports stating improvements as high as 42 percent. Property owners are also beginning to amend their leases to include the use, production or distribution of marijuana.

Which Real Estate Should You Invest In?

For now, you should be paying attention to an investment for Innovative Industrial Properties. As explained in the previous chapter, it is one of the few marijuana businesses that has consistently presented excellent stocks, and is the least likely to bomb.

There are other options available, of course, but it depends on how much you are willing to risk. I also mentioned MariMed before, but whether it's a good investment depends entirely on the outcome of the election, and whether marijuana real estate becomes a bigger deal.

Chapter 8:
The Best 3 "Not-Quite-Marijuana" Pot Stocks

Not everyone who is interested in marijuana is in it for the high. Cannabis has a ton of medical uses, so dispensaries that supply medical marijuana are vital. In fact, campaigns for medical marijuana are the biggest reason (and were the largest step forward) in state-level legalization.

It's somewhat safer to back medical marijuana than it is the recreational variety, because more states have already legalized it. Currently, 31 states are on board with prescribed medical cannabis, and forecasters believe that the number will rise by the end of the year.

However, even if it's medicinal, it is still illegal under federal law (Steiner, 2012). This is a massive problem to those who genuinely stand to benefit from marijuana's healing and pain-killing properties, and is a driving force behind the call for total legalization.

Political debate aside, there is a huge market for medical marijuana because it doesn't carry the stigma of the high life with it. More and more people are opening their minds to the scientific uses of marijuana and this has put stocks in good standing, with excellent potential for growth in the future.

Another reason why the medical sect has done so well, even in the recession when all marijuana business struggled is because it's not a matter of interest, but rather a matter of need.

People who use marijuana for their health don't have a choice but to keep the industry afloat. When dispensaries opened, it removed the need (and risk) of acquiring medical marijuana through the black market. There is ample reason to support suppliers, and so we predict that medical marijuana is here to stay and will continue on an upward path.

Of all the pot stocks to invest in, medical suppliers (or associated business) are probably the safest ones that will yield good returns now and the future. These are the top three that you should pay attention to and consider buying into:

Charlotte's Web (CWBHF)

This company has dominated the medical industry, and predictions assume that it will continue to do so for a while. It has two major factors that keep it in the lead.

Firstly, it produces CBD oil, the benefits of which are largely undisputed. The market for it is already massive and continues to expand. The reason for it is that it's low in THC (the stuff that makes you high), so it's become the preferred form of medical marijuana to many people. Remember that some people who rely on medical marijuana are of sober habits. In other cases, as with children, dosing THC is inappropriate and even dangerous.

The second perk to Charlotte's Web is that its oils are produced from hemp, which is all the rage right now in the environmental crisis. For those that don't know, hemp and marijuana are two sides of the same coin—*Cannabis sativa*—just different strains of it. Hemp is much lower in THC and therefore isn't psychoactive, it's easier to grow, and because it doesn't make people high it's considered a valuable and sustainable commodity in various industries (like clothing, paper, fuel and even food).

Even better is that in 2018 hemp became federally legal albeit with heavy and serious impositions (Hudak, 2018). This means that those who produce, distribute, sell or use hemp don't face the persecutions that marijuana businesses are under constant threat of.

Charlotte's Web, it seems, chose the right corner and set itself up for success from the very beginning. The only thing that could dampen it is the FDA, but as CBD products spread and demand increases this is unlikely to be an obstacle for much longer.

AbbVie (ABBV)

Okay, this isn't exactly a marijuana business, it's a pharmaceutical company that incorporates marijuana into its products. It's best known for Marinol—a marijuana-based medicine that eases the side effects of chemotherapy, and also helps AIDS patients with their appetite. The best part is that Marinol, unlike Charlotte's Web, is FDA approved.

AbbVie saw some difficulties in 2018, mostly due to the marijuana recession, but it made a solid comeback, and is continuing on a steady path forward. The company's shares and numbers are in fantastic standing, and because of the nature of Marinol, it's an important business that is unlikely to falter or disappear in the future.

Aleafia (ALEAF)

Aleafia isn't so well-known in the USA, but in Canada, it's one of the top marijuana facilities in the country. The company has been doing a stellar job for a while, and 2019 reports yielded numbers that are nothing short of impressive. Medical sales increased by 43 percent, while recreational sales went up by 53 percent. To top that off, the company's expenses decreased by an unbelievable 30 percent between quarters (*Aleafia Health Reports First Profitable Third Quarter*, 2019).

I should mention that Aleafia did fall victim to the recession and took quite a knock. Still, it's one of the few who recovered spectacularly, and if its 2019 reports are anything to go by, it's rapidly on the incline.

There are 65,000 patients reliant on Aleafia's services, so it's certainly got the customer base to keep it afloat for years to come.

Honorable Mentions

Don't forget that I listed a few companies dealing in the medicinal sector in chapter six. These are certainly worth investing in as well, if "not quite marijuana" is your industry of choice. To save you the effort of flipping back to them, they are:

- cbdMD

- GW Pharmaceuticals
- Truelieve Cannabis

Ancillary Pot Stocks

If you like, you don't have to invest in marijuana or any of its byproducts to buy in to pot stocks. The ancillary market is huge, and there is no risk of breaking the law as the products it produces are supplementary to marijuana but don't concern the production, use or handling of it.

Two stocks that I have already mentioned are leaders in ancillary, GrowGeneration Corp and Innovative Industrial Properties. There's one more that, alongside these two, is predicted to dominate ancillary sales and so is well worth investing in.

KushCo Holdings (KSHB)

Kushco is a branding and packaging company. It's already obvious why this is a good company to invest in. Packaging is a service that will always be required and as legalization laws open up, there'll be more reach for marijuana business to cater to. Kushco also advises marijuana companies on the legalities of how they present themselves, so it's in pretty good standing with many businesses.

Though the company does stock some marijuana products (like pre-rolls and concentrates), it does not produce the marijuana itself. Even if the market for cannabis had to completely see its backside, Kushco would still be a packaging and branding company. There is very little risk involved in investing in it.

Its numbers are excellent as well. The fourth quarter of 2019 saw a revenue increase of 135 percent, bringing in $47 million dollars (Mohazeb, 2019).

Which Market Should You Invest In?

To sum it up, buying into marijuana business as they're best known (cultivation, processing, distribution and dispensing) is the most promising, but also the riskiest of all the sectors. On the one hand, it certainly has the biggest market in terms of consumption and has laws are rewritten, there is excellent growth potential for pot stocks of this nature. However, currently federal law works against it, and this continues to cause complications in trading. The marijuana recession of 2018 affected these marijuana businesses the most and so investment options are somewhat limited as we wait for certain stocks to get back on their feet.

Medical marijuana isn't quite the same, because often the products are not psychoactive. The market may be smaller than that of recreational marijuana, but out of necessity, the demand is much more urgent and keeps the industry above water. There are fewer legal implications for investing in medical marijuana, though technically it's still federally illegal.

Marijuana real estate has some strong contenders, but the stocks depend on other marijuana businesses and the general marijuana economy. It's one of the more complicated sectors to support because administration is difficult to acquire under federal law. It's highly competitive though, and this works in many stocks' favor.

As for other ancillary stocks, they may not do as well as the rest, but they are by far the most reliable. There is no risk of legal trouble (beyond commercial and business regulation), and because these companies often supply tools to marijuana business and users alike, the market is booming.

Ultimately, the stocks you choose to buy depend on how much a risk you're willing to take. If you'd like to test the waters, I'd recommend starting with either medical marijuana or ancillary. Remember that you can invest in different sectors simultaneously as well.

Chapter 9:
If More States Legalize Marijuana in 2020, This Stock Could Be the Biggest Winner

The recession of 2018 kicked many stocks into the dirt. Some fell away, some recovered smoothly, and others are still recovering. As some of the stats I've given you have shown, 2019 was a much better year for pot stocks overall, and so forecasters predict that 2020 will be even better.

It's natural to assume that unless another curveball is thrown, the stocks that are doing well now will continue to do so. The marijuana economy is thriving well enough, and with the legalization of cannabis in Illinois, 2020 is sure to bring great things our way.

This raises the question: which stocks will benefit the most if more legalization laws see the light of day?

It's a simple question with a somewhat complicated answer because there are so many directions it could go in, and even more scenarios to consider.

Marijuana Itself Could Be the Victor

First, we have to consider how recreational marijuana will benefit the most if ever it's totally legalized. This makes sense because if the threat of persecution is removed, more consumers will freely purchase it, and more institutions (like banks) will be willing to back it. Capital will rise, production will increase, sales will improve and stocks will go up.

Investing in marijuana companies won't be as risky, and there's a good chance that those who are currently in the red or being written off will gain the power to bounce back as though nothing ever happened.

But there's still an issue or two regarding marijuana businesses, regardless of how far its legalization stretches.

First, there's one that I already mentioned: commoditization. This problem is unlikely to go away if weed is totally legalized and in fact, may even become a more pressing one. If marijuana is officially recognized as a legal and safe commodity, and if production and distribution truly become mainstream, stock value could easily plummet (remember the carrot analogy).

The second problem is that marijuana doesn't just fall from the sky. Unless the businesses are cultivating and managing it themselves, they're going to have to rely on other markets to keep going. So...

Real Estate May Be the Winner

You could have all the marijuana seeds in the world, and all the clientele lining up at your door to get a piece of you; if you don't have property to grow, process or dispense from, you won't be able to set up shop.

Marijuana real estate is one of the sectors that has shone the most. It was practically untouched by the recession, because ultimately, it's just property. However, it faces the same complications that marijuana does because of restrictive laws that hinder administration.

If these laws were to disappear, real estate is likely to boom louder than any other market.

There'll be fewer hoops of fire to jump through, and property values will likely increase (as will demand).

Ancillary Is the True Victor

Imagine if federally marijuana was made legal. There would be no stigma, no penalties for use or sale of it, and business administration would run smoothly. The businesses that produce and dispense marijuana would have a good chance of becoming commercially mainstream and so would have to make provision for that.

Compare it to the alcohol industry. To sell beer, your branding, licensing, FDA approval, packaging, shipping, advertising, and... and... and... all have to be in good standing. Remove the ancillary from alcohol, and you're left with raw beer that you'd have to drink straight out of the vat.

For this reason, ancillary is the true commercial winner, and its stocks are likely to benefit the most from more legalization throughout the country. Not only will doors open for a whole new market of paraphernalia, but also supplementary services like advertising.

Ancillary is also backed by both marijuana businesses and real estate, because it's largely the link between the two. Without ancillary, neither will get very far. It's also worth it to note that ancillary already has the head start, as it's not suppressed by the harsh rules, laws and caveats that the other two are.

However, it doesn't end there, because one critical thing has been left out of the equation. Where are you getting the marijuana from in the first place?

These Stocks Have the Most Potential

Before I give you my top pick of investment considering legalization, I must give you a couple of honorable mentions. These stocks are likely to skyrocket in success if more states accommodate them, or if in the best-case scenario, marijuana is freed from its federal chains.

I won't go into much detail, as I have already mentioned each of them, but they are, in no particular order:

- Innovative Industrial Properties is all set to continue dominating as it has. With more legalization, there'll be a greater demand for property. This company has already planted its flag and is likely to benefit the most in real estate. Remember that it also assists with administration, so the more businesses pop up, the more opportunity it will have and the safer it will become.

- Planet 13 Holdings and GrowGeneration Corp, my top two picks from earlier, are the likeliest to expand into new territory in the USA, and so are both worth mentioning again. Both are top performing in 2020 already, and there are no warning signs that they'll slow down.

- GreenThumb Industries is already growing extremely well, and with the opportunity to expand, could accelerate straight to the top. In a similar vein, The Valens Co. and Sprott Inc. are also in the running for more momentum.

- Kushco, the best ancillary stock right now needs no explanation considering the above points of how much it stands to benefit simply because it is ancillary.

All this said, would you believe me if I told you that the most promising stock—the one that has the highest growth potential upon legalization—has nothing to do with marijuana specifically? We have to consider something that's almost always left out of the equation. If you have the weed, and you have the storefront (or land), how will you get it to your customers? Therefore, the winner is:

Scott's Miracle Gro (SMG)

This company is an ancillary business in agriculture and gardening. It supplies a range of equipment for lawns, gardens, hydroponic and organic growing, and pest management. It's not necessarily a "weed" company, as most of its revenue comes from ordinary agriculturalists and horticulturalists. This does not change the fact that Scott's Miracle-Gro products are perfect for marijuana growers. I'd even go as far as to say that the marijuana industry is largely dependent on this one single enterprise to keep going.

When other marijuana businesses struggled to stay in the game, Scott's Miracle Gro had returns of 80 percent. It wasn't touched by the recession, and it's unlikely that it will be affected by changing laws, commoditization or falling stocks in the future. So far for 2020, Scott's Miracle-Gro stocks are up.

Thinking beyond business, Scott's is still the winner. The more states legalize recreational use, and the more lenient laws restriction home-growth become, the more citizens will buy into producing their own weed, expanding the already flourishing market for the company.

It seems odd that your best choice is a simple gardening brand, but it's undoubtedly the stock with the most value and potential in our changing political climate.

Why Not Kushco, Then?

You may be wondering why Kushco isn't the obvious winner if it's the best stock to pick for ancillary in the marijuana market. Good question.

The biggest reason for this is that though Kushco is a packaging and branding company, it is one that falls specifically into the marijuana market. It depends on the health of other businesses and sectors to continue, and because of this it fluctuates more than Scott's does.

Kushco has seen some struggles in the recession. Although it reported stellar numbers in 2019, and is set to grow much more in 2020, it's not as stable as Scott's because it limits itself to cannabis. The latter hasn't faltered in a long time, and is a strong business to invest in, regardless of the marijuana economy.

Still, to be fair, Kushco takes second place. If you're looking to invest in a strong future in marijuana stocks, you'd be wise to focus on these two. The way it's looking now, it's the perfect time to buy in and there is very little risk of loss associated with both.

Conclusion:
2020 Could Be the Year for You

There's not much more to it. Trading and investing in marijuana is not a difficult industry to get into, nor is it as problematic as some observers have made it seem. The truth is that other resources promote a message that pot stocks are a stupid investment and that they're unlikely to survive the coming months, year or decade.

It's not to say that you shouldn't heed any warnings, but please do take them with a grain of salt. If the marijuana industry was collapsing, failing or bombing, you'd know about it without a doubt. Yet, as you saw in this book, many of them pot stocks are going strong and doing better than they've ever done before.

What you have to realize is that the risks of trading aren't isolated to trading. In any business, whether you're selling apples at a farmer's market, producing electronic gadgets, or offering a service of some sort there will always be room for error. Products become obsolete, and customers change their minds. The economy fluctuates, and society evolves.

An entrepreneur, business person or investor has to have a sense of foresight to thrive. When it comes to trading, particularly trading marijuana, that foresight will go a long way.

The question is not whether you should invest in pot stocks, it's how are you going to? There is much risk here as there is with any other faction of trading and the naysayers are lying to you if they make it seem as though this is a dying trend.

Yes, there are some problems associated with pot stocks, but these will fall away in time. The biggest problem currently is that the industry is still new. There are bound to be some bumps in the road before it's smooth sailing, but as they say, you have to walk before you can run.

As the USA's laws progress, legalization spreads and a new generation takes over, marijuana could very well become one of the best performing stocks. It just needs time to prove itself. That said, you're not exempt from playing your part if you want to join the ranks.

Insider information is the most valuable part of trading, so wherever possible, make connections. They'll take you further than any research will, and once you have those connections you'll be able to make better business decisions when it comes to holding or selling. This will maximize your gains and minimize your losses.

However, I have said it multiple times and I will say it again: do your research. Get to know the stocks. In time, predicting their health will become easier, but it can't be taught. It's one of those things that you acquire through experience and there is no way around that. If you combine these two things, you stand a good chance of proving the aforementioned naysayers wrong.

Beyond this, it's simply a lie that 2020 isn't a good year for pot stocks. It's looking like the best year we've had so far, on multiple accounts.

Firstly, it's apparent that we've seen the back of the recession. Naturally, one is bound to hit again, but forecasters aren't predicting that we'll head through one this year. Businesses are recovering from the losses faced back then, and it seems that the creases have been ironed out.

Secondly, the market itself is growing. Recreational marijuana has made its way into the mainstream regardless of its illegal status. What the naysayers forget is that it's marijuana we're talking about. It will never go out of fashion, and even if it did, 2020 won't be the year it gets pushed out. Furthermore, other markets are booming too: real estate, branding, medical and therapeutic marijuana, and even commercially with vapes, edibles and infused drinks. With the rise of the latter, we can only assume that the market is expanding, not shrinking as so many have come to believe.

Thirdly, there's the election. We can only wait and see how it turns out, but it could be huge. Politicians are already stating their support of the industry and promising to make the necessary changes that will help marijuana businesses instead of hindering them. That ball is in our court, but it's looking good.

And finally, regardless of the previous point or federal law, legalization has finally become a priority. The USA is well on its way to total legalization, but in the meantime, more states are beginning to realize that allowing marijuana businesses to operate helps the state and the country, because it contributes to a whole number of things including tourism and the economy. As for pot stocks, the more states legalize, the wider the market becomes. This isn't just wishful thinking; this is the trend in the USA today.

So, with the dawn of the new decade, pot stocks are in. If ever it were a good idea to invest in them it would be now. So long as you do so responsibly, you have little to lose and a lot to gain from this. Speaking of which, before you run out to throw money at your chosen stocks, it would be a good idea to remember the rules:

diversify, dig deeper, and make informed decisions. Keep these in mind and before you know it, your business could boom to an all-time high.

References

Akolowala, T. (2016, July 26). When Yahoo Refused to Buy Google for $1 Million. NDTV Gadgets 360. https://gadgets.ndtv.com/internet/news/when-yahoo-refused-to-buy-google-for-1-million-865458

Aleafia Health Reports First Profitable Third Quarter. (2019). Aleafia Health. https://aleafiahealth.com/news-releases/aleafia-health-reports-first-profitable-third-quarter/

anchanaprat, N. (2017). Money Profit Finance. In Pixabay. https://pixabay.com/photos/money-profit-finance-business-2696219/

Angell, T. (2020, February 1). Bernie Sanders Pledges Legal Marijuana In All 50 States On Day One As President. Forbes. https://www.forbes.com/sites/tomangell/2020/02/01/bernie-sanders-pledges-legal-marijuana-in-all-50-states-on-day-one-as-president/#1a01ad21c166

Ardity, A. (2016). Business Stock Market. In Pixabay. https://pixabay.com/photos/business-stock-finance-market-1730089/

cnbc.com, A. B., special to. (2019, March 28). Cannabis retailer MedMen's financial troubles are a warning for the marijuana industry. CNBC. https://www.cnbc.com/2019/03/28/medmens-financial-troubles-are-a-warning-for-the-marijuana-industry.html

CNN, R. P. (2019, June 27). Illinois is expunging marijuana convictions from nearly 800,000 criminal records. CNN. https://edition.cnn.com/2019/06/27/us/illinois-expunging-marijuana-convictions-trnd/index.html

Corporation, C. G. (2019, November 11). Canopy Growth Reports Second Quarter Fiscal 2020 Financial Results. Www.Prnewswire.Com. https://www.prnewswire.com/news-releases/canopy-growth-reports-second-quarter-fiscal-2020-financial-results-300958036.html

Countries Where Weed Is Illegal 2019. (2019). Worldpopulationreview.Com. http://worldpopulationreview.com/countries/countries-where-weed-is-illegal/

Crescoli, G. (2017). Dices Over Newspaper. In Pixabay. https://pixabay.com/illustrations/dices-over-newspaper-profit-2656028/

Di Cannabis, T. (2018). Cannabis Hemp. In Pixabay. https://pixabay.com/photos/cannabis-hemp-chanvre-hanf-4688511/

Dilution, Not Bankruptcy, Is the Key Risk Facing Aurora Cannabis Stock. (2019, December 11). InvestorPlace. https://investorplace.com/2019/12/dilution-bankruptcy-key-risk-aurora-stock/

Global Cannabis Sales Grow 48% to $15 Billion in 2019. (2020, January 16). Www.Businesswire.Com. https://www.businesswire.com/news/home/2020011

6005248/en/Global-Cannabis-Sales-Grow-48-15-Billion

Gould, S., & Berke, J. (2019, June 25). States where marijuana is legal - Business Insider. Business Insider; Business Insider. https://www.businessinsider.com/legal-marijuana-states-2018-1?IR=T

GrowGeneration. (2019, November 11). GrowGeneration Reports Record Q3 2019 Revenues and Net Income. Www.Prnewswire.Com. https://www.prnewswire.com/news-releases/growgeneration-reports-record-q3-2019-revenues-and-net-income-300955053.html

Hudak, J. (2018, December 14). The Farm Bill, hemp legalization and the status of CBD: An explainer. Brookings; Brookings. https://www.brookings.edu/blog/fixgov/2018/12/14/the-farm-bill-hemp-and-cbd-explainer/

Inc, P. 13 H. (2019, November 25). Planet 13 Announces Third Quarter 2019 Financial Results. Www.Newswire.Ca. https://www.newswire.ca/news-releases/planet-13-announces-third-quarter-2019-financial-results-809953549.html

Marijuana and Real Estate: A Budding Issue. (2020). Www.Nar.Realtor. https://www.nar.realtor/reports/marijuana-and-real-estate-a-budding-issue

Medgadget. (2020, January 16). Cannabis Market 2020: Global Analysis, Share, Trends, Application Analysis and Forecast To 2026 | CBD | CBD Oil |

Sales and Consumption |. Medgadget. https://www.medgadget.com/2020/01/cannabis-market-2020-global-analysis-share-trends-application-analysis-and-forecast-to-2026-cbd-cbd-oil-sales-and-consumption.html

Medlen, R. (2016). Foliage Cannabis. In Pixabay. https://pixabay.com/photos/foliage-cannabis-marijuana-lush-1157792/

Mohazeb, N. (2019, November 8). KushCo Holdings Fourth Quarter and Full Year Financial Results. The Green Fund. https://thegreenfund.com/kushco-holdings-fourth-quarter-and-full-year-financial-results

Ndispensable. (2018). Green kush on white textile. In Unsplash. https://unsplash.com/photos/zwc6BD4_RDE

noexcusesradio. (2014a). Marijuana Colorado. In Pixabay. https://pixabay.com/photos/marijuana-colorado-marijuana-grow-269851/

Romero, D. (2019, September 20). California's cannabis black market is eclipsing its legal one. NBC News. https://www.nbcnews.com/news/us-news/california-s-cannabis-black-market-has-eclipsed-its-legal-one-n1053856

Schuba, T. (2020, January 13). 12 days, $20 million: Recreational weed sales remain high in Illinois. Chicago Sun-Times. https://chicago.suntimes.com/cannabis/2020/1/13/21064646/illinois-legal-weed-sales-totals-2020 spyglasshill. (2014b). Smoke Dude. In Pixabay. https://pixabay.com/photos/smoke-dude-boy-smoking-cigarette-484090/

Steiner, M. (2012, March 12). Medical Marijuana and Federal Law. Www.Criminaldefenselawyer.Com; Nolo. https://www.criminaldefenselawyer.com/resources/criminal-defense/federal-crime/medical-marijuana-federal-laws.htm

Valery, J. (2019). burning banknotes. In Unsplash. https://unsplash.com/photos/hfrDZAXwb5c/info

Williams, S. (2019, November 17). 6 States Trying to Legalize Recreational Marijuana in 2020. The Motley Fool; The Motley Fool. https://www.fool.com/investing/2019/11/17/6-states-trying-to-legalize-recreational-marijuana.aspx

Williams, S. (2020, February 16). Donald Trump and Marijuana: Everything You Need to Know. The Motley Fool. https://www.fool.com/investing/2020/02/16/donald-trump-and-marijuana-everything-you-need-to.aspx

www.ingramcontent.com/pod-product-compliance
Lightning Source LLC
Chambersburg PA
CBHW070940080526
44589CB00013B/1587